DISEASE
UPDATE

The **ADHD** Update
Understanding Attention-Deficit/Hyperactivity Disorder

Alvin and Virginia Silverstein and Laura Silverstein Nunn

Enslow Publishers, Inc.
40 Industrial Road
Box 398
Berkeley Heights, NJ 07922
USA
http://www.enslow.com

Acknowledgments

The authors thank Thor Bergersen, M.D., Director, Hallowell Center, Needham, MA, and Robert J. Resnick, Ph.D., ABPP, Board Certified Clinical Psychologist and Professor of Psychology, Randolph-Macon College, Ashland, VA, for their careful reading of the manuscript and their many helpful comments and suggestions.

Library of Congress Cataloging-in-Publication Data

Silverstein, Alvin.
    The ADHD update : understanding attention-deficit/hyperactivity disorder / Alvin and Virginia Silverstein and Laura Silverstein Nunn.
       p. cm. — (Disease update)
    Summary: "Introduction to the history and most up-to-date research and treatment of ADHD"—Provided by publisher.
    Includes bibliographical references and index.
    ISBN-13: 978-0-7660-2800-5
    ISBN-10: 0-7660-2800-3
    1. Attention-deficit hyperactivity disorder—Juvenile literature. I. Silverstein, Virginia B. II. Nunn, Laura Silverstein. III. Title.
    RJ506.H9S557 2008
    618.92'8589—dc22

                              2007013853

Printed in the United States of America

10 9 8 7 6 5 4 3 2 1

To Our Readers: We have done our best to make sure all Internet Addresses in this book were active and appropriate when we went to press. However, the author and the publisher have no control over and assume no liability for the material available on those Internet sites or on other Web sites they may link to. Any comments or suggestions can be sent by e-mail to comments@enslow.com or to the address on the back cover.

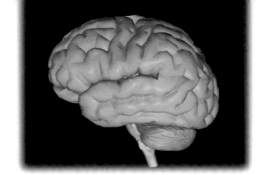

Contents

Attention-Deficit/Hyperactivity Disorder (ADHD)

What is it?
ADHD is a common behavioral condition that causes problems in three main areas: inability to focus or pay attention (inattention), being overly active (hyperactivity), and acting without thinking first (impulsivity).

Who gets it?
It is most often identified in school-age children, but many of them will continue to have the condition as adults. ADHD is diagnosed three times more often in boys than in girls.

How do you get it?
The cause of ADHD is not known. The condition may be inherited, passed from generation to generation. In rare cases it can result from damage to nerves in the brain.

What are the symptoms?
Not being able to pay attention is a main symptom. Hyperactivity is also commonly seen, especially in young children. Impulsive behavior and being easily distracted are also common.

How are the symptoms treated?

A combination of some or all of the following are usually used: behavior therapy, school counseling, social skills training, and medication. Exercise may also help to regain focus. Schools are usually involved in the treatment of ADHD students.

How can it be prevented?

Since the cause of ADHD is unknown, no one knows yet whether or not it can be prevented. Successful treatment of people with ADHD may help lessen their symptoms so that they can be more focused and less impulsive.

Atlanta Braves' first baseman Adam LaRoche was discouraged after making an error caused by his attention deficit disorder.

1

Out of Control

ON MAY 14, 2006, Atlanta Braves' first baseman Adam LaRoche made a big blunder on the field that made his baseball coaches and fans angry. It also led to some positive changes in his life. It was supposed to be a routine play—all he had to do was scoop up a ground ball and step on first base to make the third out of the inning. Simple. But what happened was not that simple. To everyone's surprise, LaRoche did not run, but slowly jogged to first, as the Washington Nationals' batter, Nick Johnson, raced down the baseline. The umpire called Johnson safe. LaRoche's mental error led to four runs that inning by the Nationals, who went on to beat the Braves 8 to 1. LaRoche took a lot of heat from fans and news reporters because of his laid-back, seemingly uncaring attitude. But if it looked like his head wasn't in the game, he didn't mean to be that way—he actually has attention deficit disorder (ADD for short).

Growing up, LaRoche had always had trouble paying attention. His mind would often drift off, causing him to forget what task he was supposed to be doing. Many people thought he was lazy. When LaRoche was in high school, a doctor diagnosed him with ADD, but LaRoche did not take it seriously. He did not want to use ADD as an excuse for things that he did or did not do, so he didn't do anything about it.

When LaRoche started playing minor league baseball, the coaches noticed that he did not seem to be trying hard. They thought he was too laid-back and inattentive to be an athlete. They told him to try to at least look like he was excited about playing baseball. It wasn't that simple. Even after LaRoche made it to the big leagues, he continued to have trouble focusing. Sometimes he would forget how many outs there were, so he had to keep looking at the scoreboard. And sometimes he had to be reminded when it was his turn to bat.

In 2003, LaRoche tried taking an ADD drug, Ritalin, to treat his condition, but he kept forgetting to take his pills. He did not notice any improvement—probably because he was not taking the medication regularly—so after two weeks he stopped taking the drug at all. When he made that blunder in May 2006, the pressure from the fans and the coaches made him realize that he needed to take a serious look at his condition. Was it really ADD that was causing him to make these mistakes? Until then, he hadn't been convinced that this condition was at the root of his problems on the field.

The following month, LaRoche went to see a doctor who specialized in ADD and ADHD (attention-deficit/hyperactivity disorder). He asked the doctor, "Do I have ADD, or am I using this as my excuse to be a lazy human being?"[1] LaRoche was given extensive psychological testing that involved gathering information about his behaviors in various situations (school, home, activities) during childhood as well as in the present. When the tests were completed, his doctor told him, "One hundred percent, without a doubt, you have attention deficit disorder, and you need something to make your brain function like everybody else's."[2] LaRoche was worried about how the medicine would make him feel. Would it turn him into a different person? The doctor prescribed a low dose of a Ritalin-like drug and assured LaRoche that it would not change his personality. It would just help his brain to focus better.

A couple of weeks after LaRoche started taking the ADD medicine, he could feel the difference. "It helps me to focus for three hours when I'm playing and not be spacing out or thinking about a million different things," he explained in an interview.[3] His wife, Jennifer, also noticed differences in his behavior both on the field and at home. Some of his teammates even came up to him before they knew he was taking medication and asked him if he was taking something. They told him that he seemed more awake and had more energy. Many other people had commented that they noticed a change in his behavior as well. For the first time, at age twenty-six, LaRoche felt like he finally had some control, and it showed on the field. His game-playing skills improved dramatically. From May 14 to July 16, LaRoche's batting average went up 38 points. By early August, he had already hit more home runs than he had the whole season before.[4]

When people think of ADD, they often picture out-of-control kids who can't sit still and get into trouble a lot. Adam LaRoche does not seem to fit that typical image. He is not a kid—he is in his mid-twenties.

After LaRoche started treatment for his ADD, his batting average improved dramatically.

He does not have too *much* energy, he has a *lack* of it. Attention deficit disorder (ADD)—LaRoche's condition—is one kind of attention disorder. People with ADD are unable to keep focused on one activity for long.

Many people with attention disorders have two other symptoms as well: They are bursting with energy and have difficulty sitting still (hyperactivity), and they have trouble controlling their actions (impulsivity). The term *attention-deficit/hyperactivity disorder (ADHD)* is now used for the whole group of attention disorders. It includes people with or without hyperactivity.

ADHD is a common disorder that affects at least 2 million school-age children in the United States. In a class of about thirty children, chances are at least one of them will have ADHD. Not all kids with ADHD will grow out of it as they get older. In fact, like Adam LaRoche, a lot of kids with ADHD—as many as 70 percent—continue to show symptoms as teenagers and adults.[5]

People with ADHD, whether they are hyperactive or quiet, have a hard time controlling their behavior. Kids may have trouble learning in school, behaving at home, or making and keeping friends. Adults may also have problems with friends and family, and they may not be able to keep a job for very long. As a result, many

Hyperactive Kids

ADHD used to be called hyperactivity. The word *hyper* means "too much." A hyperactive child is more active than most kids. He or she usually has trouble sitting still. Hyperactive kids often fidget, rock back and forth, or suddenly jump up and run around.

people with ADHD often feel like they are bad or stupid. The truth is, their brains just work differently than most people's. Fortunately, ADHD can be treated. There are medicines that, when

> ADHD is a common disorder that affects at least 2 million school-age children in the United States. In a class of about thirty children, chances are at least one of them will have ADHD.

taken daily, can help people sit still and focus better. People can also learn how to control their behavior through behavior therapy (treatment involving techniques to help change behaviors). With proper treatment, people with ADHD can gain control over their lives and feel better about themselves.

DER STRUWWELPETER

von
Dr. Heinr. Hoffmann

Sieh einmal, hier steht er.
Pfui! Der *Struwwelpeter!*
An den Händen beiden
Ließ er sich nicht schneiden
Seine Nägel fast ein Jahr;
Kämmen ließ er nicht sein
Haar.
Pfui! Ruft da ein jeder:
Garst'ger Struwwelpeter!

Heinrich Hoffmann's book, published in 1845, contained many poems of children who misbehaved. *Der Struwwelpeter* means "Slovenly Peter."

2

The History of ADHD

GERMAN PSYCHIATRIST Heinrich Hoffmann became well known when he published a book of poems he wrote and illustrated for children in 1845. His collection of poems described children who misbehave, most likely based on his observations of young patients he had treated. Originally, Hoffmann had written and illustrated these stories as a Christmas gift for his three-year-old son before he decided to publish them.

Today, medical experts believe that Heinrich Hoffmann's writings of misbehaving children, especially in his poem "The Story of Fidgety Philip," gave the first accurate description of what we now call attention-deficit/hyperactivity disorder (ADHD).[1]

The Story of Fidgety Philip

"Let me see if Philip can
Be a little gentleman;
Let me see if he is able
To sit still for once at the table."
Thus Papa bade Phil behave;
And Mama looked very grave.
But Fidgety Phil,
He won't sit still;
He wriggles,
And giggles,
And then, I declare,
Swings backwards and forwards,
And tilts up his chair,
Just like any rocking horse—
"Philip! I am getting cross!"

See the naughty, restless child
Growing still more rude and wild,
Till his chair falls over quite.
Philip screams with all his might,
Catches at the cloth, but then
That makes matters worse again.
Down upon the ground they fall,
Glasses, plates, knives, forks and all.
How Mama did fret and frown,
When she saw them tumbling down!
And Papa made such a face!
Philip is in sad disgrace. . . .[2]

Recognizing an Age-Old Problem

Dr. Heinrich Hoffmann may have been the first person to give an accurate description of ADHD, but this was surely not a new condition. Extremely fidgety, overactive kids had been around since long before the 1800s—probably for as long as children have been around. And throughout history, kids who "misbehaved" were often treated very badly. Centuries ago, many people believed that hyperactive behavior was caused by demons taking over a person's body—or else it was a punishment by the gods. Well into modern times, it was commonly believed that a child's unacceptable behavior was simply the result of poor parenting. Too often, these children were punished with severe beatings.

ADHD was not recognized as a medical condition until the early 1900s.

While ADHD may have been around a long time, it was not recognized as a medical condition until the early 1900s. In 1902, English pediatrician George Still presented a series of lectures to the Royal College of Physicians. He discussed behavior problems in a group of forty-three children he treated in his medical practice. He described these children as defiant, aggressive, resistant to discipline, lawless, overly emotional, passionate, and having little "inhibitory volition" (control of their actions).[3] Basically, these kids had little or no awareness of their destructive behavior. Most of the children in this group were boys, and the alarming behaviors were noticeable before the age of eight.

Dr. Still was surprised to learn that most of the kids came from "good homes," so it did not seem that their destructive behaviors resulted from bad parenting. He thought that the problem was more biological than it was psychological. He suspected that the condition was either inherited or caused by brain damage at birth. Dr. Still also found out that some of the children's family members had other psychiatric problems such as depression, alcoholism, or conduct problems.

Dr. Still's ideas had a big impact on the medical community. Medical experts started to change their way of thinking. They realized that perhaps these children were not bad or evil. In the years that followed, researchers continued to study this behavioral condition in hopes of finding kinder, more effective methods of treatment.

In the 1920s, researchers discovered that a number of children had developed behavior problems after

English pediatrician George Still, pictured here, helped ADHD to be recognized as a medical condition by giving a series of lectures to the Royal College of Physicians. Below is the crest of the Royal College of Physicians.

COLL:REG:MED

having encephalitis (a viral infection of the brain) during a major outbreak in 1917–1918. These children were hyperactive, lacked control over their actions, and had a very short attention span—the same behavior problems that Dr. Still had described years earlier. Doctors felt that these behaviors were caused by brain damage. Children who showed these symptoms were labeled "brain damaged." Even if they had not had encephalitis, they were still called brain damaged. Eventually, however, doctors realized that many of the children were actually quite smart. How could their brains work so well if they were damaged? There must be some other cause for hyperactive behavior.

Discovering Treatments

In 1937, American physician Charles Bradley discovered the first effective treatment for ADHD quite by accident. He was trying to find a drug that would ease spinal tap headaches in children. (A spinal tap is a procedure that removes fluid from the spinal column. A common side effect is a really bad headache.) He noticed that one drug he tried, Benzedrine, did little to help the headaches, but seemed to calm some of his patients who had behavior problems. In fact, teachers reported that a

The Name Game

Over the last one hundred years, ADHD has gone through a number of name changes. The name seemed to change whenever researchers learned new information about the condition. When brain damage was believed to be a cause, the condition was called minimal brain damage (MBD), and later minimal brain dysfunction. It has also been commonly called hyperactivity, because a telltale sign of the condition was being overactive.

In 1980, the American Psychiatric Association added the name *attention deficit disorder* (ADD) to their official list, to focus on the lack of attention. This could occur either with or without hyperactivity. The name was changed again in 1994 to attention-deficit/hyperactivity disorder (ADHD), which was used to describe a condition with inattention, hyperactivity, or a combination of both. Some mental health experts are uncomfortable with the term *disorder* in ADHD, since it suggests that there is something "wrong." They think that the brains of people with ADHD just work *differently*. It seems likely that ADHD will go through more name changes in the future.

number of the children showed great improvement in their behavior and learning in the classroom. Some of the kids even called the medication "math pills" because they were having an easier time learning math. (This subject used to be very difficult for them.) When the children stopped taking the medication, however, their teachers noticed that the old behaviors returned.

Dr. Bradley found the results very surprising because Benzedrine is a stimulant—a drug that normally raises the heart rate, blood pressure, and activity level. He did not understand why the stimulant seemed to calm hyperactive children.

Searching for a Cause

Despite Dr. Bradley's promising findings, stimulants were not used much to treat hyperactive children until the 1950s and 1960s. In 1955, the Food and Drug Administration (FDA) approved the stimulant methylphenidate (brand name Ritalin) to treat a number of psychological disorders, which did not yet include ADHD.

In 1960, New York child psychiatrist Stella Chess coined the term *Hyperactive Child Syndrome*. In a research paper, she described a hyperactive child as "one who carries out activities at a higher than normal rate of speed than the average child, or who is constantly in motion, or both."[4] Some of her hyperactive patients had obvious causes for their behavior: brain damage, mental retardation, extreme stress in their environment, or a serious mental illness. But many of them—thirty-seven out of eighty-two—had no past problems other than their hyperactive behavior.[5] Other experts at the time believed that hyperactivity was caused by bad parenting or toxins (poisons) in the environment. Chess, however, felt that hyperactivity was due to something different in the workings of the brain. She recommended a combined approach to treatment, including behavior therapy, medication, special education in the schools, active involvement of the parents, and psychotherapy if the child's hyperactive behavior had resulted in psychological problems.

The research of Chess and others began to change psychiatrists' views of hyperactive children and how they should be treated. By 1967, Ritalin was being prescribed specifically to treat children with hyperactivity. Using stimulants to treat this condition soon became increasingly common.

The hyperactivity disorder stirred up a lot of controversy. Not everybody could agree on what caused it, let alone how to treat it. In 1973, Dr. Benjamin Feingold, a pediatrician and allergist, had a different theory on the cause of hyperactivity. He believed that food additives, preservatives, and artificial colorings were to blame for making kids overactive. He also suggested that eating too much sugar could bring on the

Dr. Benjamin Feingold believed that sugar and other food additives caused hyperactivity disorder.

condition. He recommended that parents reduce the amount of sugar their children ate. He offered a special diet that did not include food colorings or any other artificial chemicals. He also recommended other foods that contained natural chemicals called salicylates. These substances, chemically related to aspirin, can be found in everyday foods such as almonds, cucumbers, tomatoes, apples, and berries.

Dr. Feingold found that up to 50 percent of children who stuck to his recommended diet showed improvement.[6] Many parents welcomed this new diet as a safe alternative to medication. The National Institute of Mental Health (NIMH) conducted a number of independent studies on the effect of a restricted diet on hyperactivity. In 1982, the NIMH announced that such a diet helped only about 5 percent of hyperactive children—mostly young children with food allergies.[7]

During the 1970s, doctors started to realize that some adults had attention problems, too. Researchers interviewed their parents and childhood teachers and found that the adults in question had shown typical signs of hyperactivity as children, but had gone undiagnosed.

In 1990, NIMH researcher Alan Zametkin and his team conducted a study to find out if the brains of people with ADD worked differently from those of people in the general population. The study team used a positron-emission tomography (PET) scan, in which a radioactive form of glucose (a sugar) was injected into the subjects. (The amount of radiation given to the subjects was very small—not enough to harm them.) On PET scans, areas of the brain that are working actively take up the radioactive sugar and show up as bright spots. Scans were taken of adults with attention problems and a similar group without any symptoms of ADD. The brain scans of the two groups looked quite different. In people without attention problems, certain areas in the scan were brightly lit, but in those with ADD symptoms, the same areas showed up as dim or dark. For example, there was less brain activity in

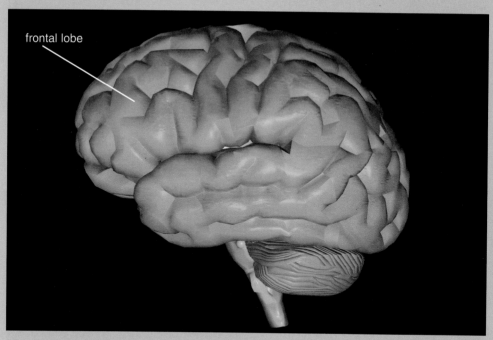

frontal lobe

In Dr. Zametkin's study, people with ADD had less activity in the frontal lobe of their brain.

the frontal lobe (in the forehead) in people with ADD. The frontal lobe of the brain is involved in attention and self-control. Many medical experts felt that these findings indicated that ADD was indeed a medical condition.

In 1999, the *American Journal of Psychiatry* published the results of the largest study on ADHD treatment in history. It was called the Multimodal Treatment Study of Children with ADHD, or MTA for short. This study, sponsored by the NIMH, went on for fourteen months and involved nearly 600 school-children, aged seven to nine, diagnosed with ADHD. The purpose of the study was to find out which type of ADHD treatment was most effective: 1) medication alone, 2) behavioral treatment alone, 3) a combination of both, or 4) routine community care. The last group allowed parents to decide which treatments were best for their children. Most of the children in this group received medication prescribed by their family doctors. Typically, these children received lower doses of drugs such as Ritalin than those in group 1.

Early findings showed that either medication alone or a combination of medication with behavioral treatment (groups 1 and 3) was much more effective in reducing ADHD symptoms than strictly behavioral treatments alone or community care. A rather surprising result was that the children treated with medication (alone or with behavioral treatment) improved greatly in social skills as well. They cooperated better with their parents and classmates. The researchers concluded that treating ADHD eliminated the symptoms that had kept children from learning social skills. Researchers continued to publish follow-up reports in the following years based on this large study. They are continuing to observe the children through adolescence to track long-term effects of the early treatment.[8]

3

What Is ADHD?

AS THE AUTHOR AND ILLUSTRATOR OF popular children's books, including the *Captain Underpants* series, Dav Pilkey knows how to get kids excited about reading. What kid could resist potty humor and booger jokes in such books as *Captain Underpants and the Attack of the Talking Toilets* or *Captain Underpants and the Perilous Plot of Professor Poopypants*? But Dav's books are more than just silly bathroom humor—kids can really relate to them. Two characters in particular, George Beard and Harold Hutchins, do rather poorly in school, and they often find themselves getting into trouble with their teachers and school principal. Their adventures are more than just stories; they are actually based on Dav's

Many children enjoy reading Dav Pilkey's books.

own experiences growing up. When he was young, Dav Pilkey was diagnosed with attention-deficit/hyperactivity disorder.

Dav Pilkey has loved to draw for almost his entire life. As a little kid, he spent a lot of time drawing animals, monsters, and superheroes. He was pretty happy doing his own thing. When Dav started kindergarten, he learned how much fun it was to make people laugh. He was really good at making funny noises and seeing how many crayons he could stick up his nose. Unfortunately, his teacher didn't think he was very funny. She found him disruptive and sent him to the principal's office on a regular basis. He spent so much time in the principal's office that his parents finally had to seek professional help to find out why Dav couldn't behave in school. It was then that Dav was diagnosed with learning and reading problems, as well as attention-deficit/hyperactivity disorder.

Dav continued to have a tough time in school. In first grade, he was known as a class clown. His teacher didn't like his kind of humor, so she sent him out of the classroom regularly. Eventually, she moved a desk out into the hallway for him. Dav used this time to make his own little comic books from a supply of paper, pencils, and crayons that he had stuffed into the hallway desk before class. One of the characters he created was Captain Underpants. Everybody in his class loved his silly superheroes—except for his teacher. One day, she actually ripped up one of his books and told him that he needed to take life more seriously, rather than spending his time making "silly books." He didn't listen to her, though.

High school was not much better for Dav. His teachers did not like his sense of humor, nor did they encourage his artistic talents. Things changed in college, though. One of Dav's professors told him that she liked his creative writing skills, and she encouraged him to write books. This is when Dav wrote his first book, *World War Won*, which won a contest and later got published.[1]

Through his books, Dav tries to encourage kids who struggle in school like he did. "I try to get the point across that not everybody thinks the same way," he explains. "Try to remember that being unsuccessful in school doesn't automatically mean you'll be unsuccessful in life. Lots of people who didn't excel in school still went on to have successful lives. For example, Thomas

Thomas Edison

Some Famous People With ADHD

Many people with ADHD are very smart and creative. They have become teachers, doctors, lawyers, inventors, movie stars, company presidents, or athletes. Although the condition may not have been officially diagnosed, some historians and psychologists believe that a number of famous people—past and present—have had ADHD. They base this view on studies of their behavior patterns.

Name	Occupation
Alexander Graham Bell	Inventor
Ludwig van Beethoven	Composer
Terry Bradshaw	Football player/sports analyst
Jim Carrey	Actor/comedian
Cher	Singer/actress
Walt Disney	Cartoonist
Thomas Edison	Inventor
Albert Einstein	Physicist
Dwight D. Eisenhower	General, U.S. president
Benjamin Franklin	Politician, inventor, scientist
Dustin Hoffman	Actor
Wolfgang Amadeus Mozart	Composer
Pablo Picasso	Artist
Ty Pennington	TV personality (*Extreme Makeover: Home Edition*)
Suzanne Somers	Actress
Steven Spielberg	Filmmaker
Robin Williams	Actor/comedian

Edison's teachers thought he was retarded . . . but he ended up doing pretty well for himself."[2]

Behavior Problems

Attention-deficit/hyperactivity disorder, or ADHD for short, is a condition in which people have trouble controlling their behavior in different settings, such as at home or in school. All children have behavior problems at times. Children with ADHD have problems that are extreme and occur more often than in most children.

People who have ADHD may sometimes seem like they are "spaced out"—they don't seem to listen to what

Are You Bored?

Everybody gets bored sometimes. It's no surprise if your mind wanders while you are sitting on a bench waiting for your turn to play ball, or reading a chapter in a textbook. People with ADHD, however, have a lot of trouble dealing with boredom. They feel a need to be constantly doing something. That is why it is often difficult for kids with ADHD to be calm and attentive when they need to—for example, when sitting quietly during a classroom lecture. Adults with ADHD, such as Adam LaRoche, can become so distracted in boring situations that they fail to do their jobs properly.

is said. Sometimes they may seem unfriendly, strange, too talkative, or mean. That is why some kids with ADHD have trouble making and keeping friends. They

Attention-deficit/hyperactivity disorder, or ADHD for short, is a condition in which people have trouble controlling their behavior in different settings, such as at home or in school.

are often fun to be around because they have a lot of imaginative ideas and a great sense of humor, but it can be hard to spend a lot of time with them.

Kids with ADHD may also have trouble getting along with their own family. They may not listen to their parents, or they may fight with their siblings all the time. In school, teachers find them disruptive and may think they are not very smart. Actually, most children with ADHD have at least average intelligence or higher. However, about 40 to 60 percent of them have other learning problems and do poorly in school.[3] They do have the ability to learn, but many of them have trouble focusing long enough to do their schoolwork. It is hard

Many students can get frustrated when they have trouble concentrating on their schoolwork.

for them to focus long enough to take tests or do long writing assignments, so they get poor grades.

Eventually, kids with ADHD may feel as though they can no longer relate to the people in their lives. This can make them feel sad and lonely. They don't feel good about themselves, and they may develop low self-esteem. Kids with ADHD really do want to get along with their friends, family, and teachers, but they do not realize when they are saying or doing something

What Is It Like to Have ADHD?

If you don't have ADHD, try to imagine what it feels like. First, turn on the TV and the radio. Then ask a friend to talk to you. While all this is going on, sit down and try to do your homework. Can you tune out all the distractions and do your homework? Can you talk to your friend without paying attention to the TV or radio? Some people with ADHD have trouble sorting out the many sounds, sights, and thoughts that demand attention. They do not know how to focus on just one thing at a time and tune out the rest. One person with ADHD described how it felt when he tried to do something as simple as read a book: "My thoughts raced round and round in my head. It's like my mind was a pinball machine with five or six balls smashing into each other."[4]

inappropriate. Often they are surprised when their behaviors upset or annoy other people.

Who Has ADHD?

Children as young as three years old may show symptoms of ADHD, but their parents may think they just have a lot of energy. The symptoms are likely to be noticed around school age, when kids are expected to follow rules and control their behavior.

For many years, scientists believed that only children have ADHD. They thought kids just "grew out of it" before they became adults. They now know that this is not always true.

Adults with ADHD are not usually hyperactive. That may be why doctors used to think that kids grow out of it. Adults with ADHD often have trouble paying attention and may act quickly, without thinking. They may also have trouble with relationships and have a hard time finishing projects. They may have low self-esteem, just like kids with ADHD, because they have trouble controlling their behavior.

People with ADHD often have family members—parents, grandparents, aunts, uncles, brothers or sisters, or cousins—who also have ADHD.

Types of ADHD

Not everyone with ADHD behaves the same way. In fact, ADHD symptoms can vary a great deal. Some people are full of energy and can't sit still. Others are calm, but they can't concentrate and have trouble paying attention. That's why experts often talk about three kinds of ADHD: *hyperactive-impulsive type*, *inattentive type*, and *combined type*.

Not everyone with ADHD behaves the same way. In fact, ADHD symptoms can vary a great deal. Some people are full of energy and can't sit still. Others are calm, but they can't concentrate and have trouble paying attention.

Hyperactive-impulsive type. Hyperactive kids are full of energy and always seem to be on the go. They are often fidgety and squirm in their seats. They may run around, touching or playing with whatever they see. They may have a hard time sitting still for a story or during a classroom lesson. They may talk constantly when they are supposed to be listening. Hyperactive teenagers and adults are not as obvious as kids. They may feel restless on the *inside*. They often need to keep themselves busy and try to do several things at once.

Impulsive kids do not always think before they speak or act. They often blurt out things that are inappropriate, such as commenting negatively on how someone looks. They also have trouble waiting their turn, such as during a game. They may frequently interrupt other people. They may grab a toy from another child or start hitting when they don't get what they want right away. Impulsive teenagers and adults may also act quickly and without thinking. While driving, for example, they may zip through traffic, weaving from lane to lane. They may stop suddenly or turn without signaling beforehand. They react without thinking about the effects their actions might have on other people.

Inattentive type. This type is often called attention deficit disorder (ADD). People with ADD have trouble paying attention. Their minds are often filled with so many thoughts and ideas that it is hard for them to concentrate on any one thing. They may get bored with a task after just a few minutes and start thinking about something else. Sometimes, though, if they are doing something they like, such as playing video games, they may not have any trouble paying attention. However, they may find it difficult to organize and complete a task or to focus on learning something new.

Kids with ADD are rarely hyperactive or impulsive, and yet they also have trouble learning in school. They are too busy daydreaming and often seem spaced out. They may sit quietly and seem to be working, but they are easily confused and may have trouble understanding what they are supposed to do. They find it hard to keep track of things and become distracted easily. They often forget to write down homework assignments, or they leave the assignment at school. They might forget to bring their schoolbook home, or they'll bring home the wrong one. Doing homework is especially difficult. Since people with ADD have a hard time focusing, they often make careless mistakes and have trouble finishing projects. When their homework is finally completed, it is full of errors. The same thing happens when they take tests.

Kids with ADD seem to get along better with friends, family, and teachers than those with hyperactivity and impulsivity do. For this reason, their condition often goes undiagnosed.

Combined type. Some people with ADHD show both inattentive and hyperactive-impulsive symptoms. They

Boys Versus Girls

Boys are up to three times more likely to be diagnosed with ADHD than girls, but that doesn't mean it is rare in girls. Boys tend to have the hyperactive-impulsive type. They get noticed because they are bursting with energy and often get into trouble at school. Girls, on the other hand, are more likely to have the inattentive type (ADD). They are likely to go unnoticed because they are low-key and quiet in class. If they are hyperactive, girls typically express their extra energy in different ways than boys. For example, they may be very talkative, and people think they are "too chatty."

are easily distracted and have trouble finishing projects. They are also fidgety and impulsive. Their behavior may change from day to day—they may be quiet and dreamy one day and bubbling over with energy the next.

What Causes ADHD?

Scientists have learned a lot about ADHD since the 1960s. They know it is not caused by poor parenting or teaching. Many people still think that eating too much sugar can make kids hyperactive. However, studies have shown that most cases of ADHD are not caused by a high-sugar diet. (Eating a high-protein breakfast instead of sugary foods, on the other hand, has been found to help the brains of kids with ADHD work better.) Most experts believe that ADHD occurs when part of a person's brain doesn't work as well as it should.

Each part of your brain has a special job to do. The outermost layer of the brain is called the cerebral cortex. You use it to think, remember, and make decisions. You also use it to understand and form words and to control body movements. The cerebral cortex receives messages from your ears, eyes, nose, taste buds, and skin and lets you know what is going on in the world around you.

> Most experts believe that ADHD occurs when part of a person's brain doesn't work as well as it should.

Deeper inside the brain there is a kind of relay station that contains billions of nerve cells. These nerve cells receive messages from all over the body and send out messages that control body activities. Chemicals called neurotransmitters help carry these messages from one part of the brain to another. Whenever you concentrate on something—whether it's homework or playing catch with your friends—nerve cells fire off messages back and forth at very high speeds. This fast-paced action makes it possible for you to block out

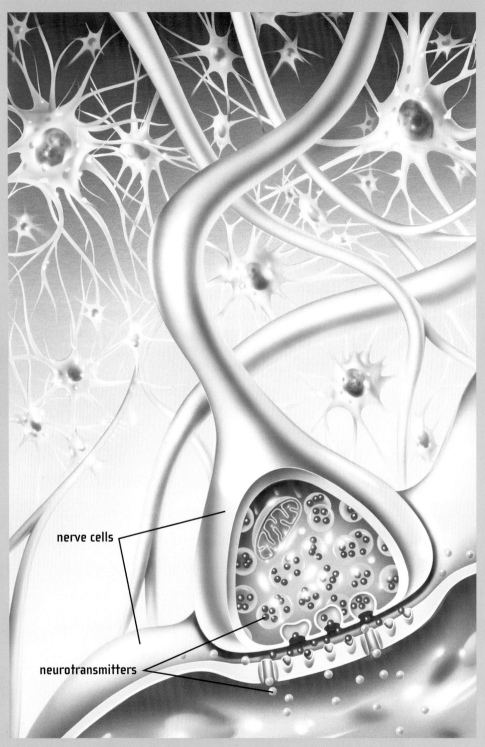

nerve cells

neurotransmitters

Neurotransmitters send signals between nerve cells. They carry messages from one part of the brain to another.

distractions and focus on what you are doing. A healthy balance of neurotransmitters helps to keep the different parts of the brain working properly.

The part of the brain right behind your forehead is called the frontal lobe. It helps you pay attention, focus on one task at a time, make plans and stick to them, and think before you act. In many people with ADHD, some structures in the frontal area are smaller than usual. As a result, the nerve cells in this area can't pick up enough of two important neurotransmitters known as dopamine and norepineph-rine. At the same time, some nerve cells grab the neurotransmitters before they reach the places where they are needed.

> Low levels of important neurotransmitters—dopamine and norepinephrine—may explain the main types of ADHD behaviors.

Norepinephrine helps a person block out distractions and focus his or her attention. When too little norepinephrine is moving through the brain, a person has trouble focusing on one thing. Dopamine helps people control their actions. If too little dopamine is flowing through the brain, a person may act impulsively—shouting out, grabbing things, or even poking a stranger who walks by. Low levels of these important neurotransmitters may thus explain the main types of ADHD behaviors.

Why does this happen? No one knows for sure, but scientists believe that ADHD is inherited—people are born with the condition. The way the brain works is determined by genes, similar to the genes that control inherited traits such as eye color and height. In people with ADHD, the genes that control the way the brain uses neurotransmitters do not work in the same way as they do in other people. Researchers have found, for example, that many people with ADHD have a particular gene for dopamine receptors in their brain cells. (Receptors are chemicals on the cell surface that pick up neurotransmitters and other chemicals.) In such people, some of the nerve cells in the frontal area of the brain, which control behavior, cannot pick up enough dopamine. The amounts of norepinephrine may also vary. Too much norepinephrine can make a person hyperactive; with too little, a person has trouble focusing on one thing at a time.

Researchers who studied identical twins—siblings who share the exact same genes—were able to show a

> Scientists believe that ADHD is inherited—people are born with the condition.

Adding to the Problem

As if ADHD weren't enough to handle, about two-thirds of kids with ADHD have other difficulties, as well. These conditions may affect mood, behavior, and learning in school.[5] Some of the most common ones include the following:

- Learning disabilities. Some children with ADHD have additional problems with reading, writing, grammar, and/or mathematics.

- Depression. These children may feel stupid, isolated, and have low self-esteem because of their problems at school, at home, and with friends.

- Anxiety. These children worry a lot and have an overwhelming sense of fear or panic. Anxiety can lead to physical symptoms, which may include a racing heart, sweating, and stomach pains.

- Severe behavior problems. These children (mostly boys) are rebellious, disruptive, stubborn, and lose their temper easily. They often argue with adults and refuse to do as they are told. Some of them are likely to get into trouble at school or with the police. They lie, steal, start fights, or bully other kids. They are aggressive toward people and/or animals, destroy others' property, break into people's cars or homes, or carry or use weapons. They are also more likely to abuse alcohol and illegal drugs.

strong link between genes and ADHD. They found that a child whose identical twin has ADHD has a much greater chance of having ADHD than does a non-twin brother or sister.

A small number of ADHD cases have been linked to other possible causes. For example, a mother who drinks alcohol, smokes cigarettes, or takes drugs during her pregnancy may damage the developing brain of an unborn child. During this time, nerve cells are making important connections, and harmful substances can interfere with this development. Too much alcohol during pregnancy may cause fetal alcohol syndrome (FAS), a condition that can lead to a low weight at birth and mental and physical defects. Many children with FAS are hyperactive, impulsive, and have difficulty paying attention, much like children with ADHD. Toxins (poisons) in the environment, such as the lead in the paint used in old buildings, have been found to cause ADHD symptoms in a few cases. Industrial chemicals, such as PCBs, can be harmful as well. (PCBs are commonly found in water and air pollution.)

4

Diagnosis and Treatment

WHEN MOLLY ZAMETKIN was in the first grade, her parents and teachers became worried about her behavior in school. She wasn't hyperactive, disruptive, or out of control. Actually, she was quite the opposite. She was quiet and often distracted. In a student evaluation requested by Molly's parents, her teacher wrote: "Her mind seems to wander in the middle of a task and during instruction. Molly is easily distracted during math—particularly when [working] in small groups."[1] Molly's father recognized the signs of attention deficit disorder (ADD). This was something he was very familiar with, considering he was Dr. Alan Zametkin, a well-known research psychiatrist at the National Institute of Mental

Health (NIMH). Dr. Zametkin had years of experience identifying the symptoms in other children. However, Molly refused to believe that *she* had ADD. She didn't want to become just another one of her dad's "mental patients."[2] In fact, it took years before Molly finally accepted her diagnosis.

At first, Molly's parents tried to treat her symptoms with behavior modification, using techniques that help to change behaviors. For some time, Molly refused to

It took a long time before Molly Zametkin was willing to accept her ADD diagnosis.

take any medication. She felt that would be like admitting she had the disorder. At the end of third grade, when Molly was still having attention problems, her parents took her to see a psychiatrist. He prescribed Dexedrine, a stimulant drug. Molly's work in school improved. Her parents and teachers noticed that she seemed to be more focused and less distractible. Molly herself was still fighting the ADD label, refusing to admit that she had a medical problem.

Eventually, the drug stopped working, so the doctor switched her prescription to a different stimulant, Concerta. By eighth grade, Molly began to realize that learning seemed easier when she was taking her medicine. Her mother no longer had to remind her to take her pills.

It wasn't until her freshman year of high school that Molly finally started to accept the fact that she did indeed have ADD. Her high school schedule was packed with classes, and after school she had two hours of lacrosse or field hockey practice. After the long days, she still had to do two to three hours of homework. She started to become more aware of her behavior, noticing that sometimes she had a lot of trouble paying attention in her afternoon classes. She worked hard despite her challenges. By the end of the school year, she was happy to see that she had done well in her classes.

Until her sophomore year of high school, Molly did not tell anybody about her ADD. She didn't want anyone to feel uncomfortable hanging out with her, knowing that she needed medication to help her pay attention. Then one day, Molly found out that her friend Jenny (not her real name) also had ADD. Jenny told Molly that she was not playing her best in field hockey practice because she had forgotten to take her Adderall that day. (Adderall was a different stimulant used to treat ADD.) Jenny told Molly that since she had started taking Adderall a few months before, she noticed that her grades and attention level were better than they had ever been.

Molly was surprised to see how Jenny's friends seemed to accept Jenny even after they found out about her condition. She thought that maybe her friends would feel the same way about her. She decided to tell them that she had ADD. Meanwhile, her doctor switched her medication to Adderall. From that point on, everything changed. She changed her attitude about school. She changed her study habits and followed techniques to get better organized. She started doing homework as soon as it was assigned rather than waiting until the last minute. She took a lot more notes and was able to focus better than she ever had. She also started to exercise and got into good physical shape. Molly's parents were very proud of the progress that she had made. In high school she had four straight years on the honor roll. And when she graduated, her grade point average was 3.9 out of 4.[3]

Is It Really ADHD?

Everybody is hyperactive, impulsive, or inattentive from time to time. That doesn't mean that they have ADHD.

Is ADHD Overdiagnosed?

In the United States, ADHD has become so common that many people think the condition is being overdiagnosed. Medical experts disagree. They say that because scientists have learned a lot about ADHD in recent years, doctors are now better able to identify it. While some cases may be misdiagnosed, many cases actually go undiagnosed. People who have ADD—without the hyperactivity—often go unnoticed because they are quietly daydreaming in the classroom. Many of them are girls like Molly Zametkin. Molly's condition might have gone undiagnosed for many years if her father had not been an expert in identifying the symptoms.

There are times when people blurt out things they didn't mean to say, start a new task before finishing an old one, or become disorganized and forgetful. Who hasn't had these things happen to them at one time or another? So how do specialists know whether a person has ADHD or is just energetic?

There is no actual test that can diagnose ADHD. High-tech brain scans, such as MRI and PET scans, can give a view of the working parts of the brain. Such scans can detect differences in brain activity, but they cannot determine whether or not a person has ADHD. Changes in brain activity may be signs of other brain disorders. Therefore, brain scans are not widely used as a diagnostic tool. For children and teenagers, a diagnosis must be based on symptoms observed by parents, teachers, and a school counselor or mental health professional. Adults often seek help on their own because they are having problems in their work or their relationships with other people.

> Everybody is hyperactive, impulsive, or inattentive from time to time. That doesn't mean that they have ADHD.

In many cases, a primary care doctor can make a diagnosis. A physical exam is usually a good way to start. Tests for hearing and vision may be given as well, to rule out other medical conditions. The doctor will also ask a lot of questions. What is the patient's medical history? Does the patient get along well with other people? How does he or she behave at home and at school or work? How long has the patient been behaving this way? How does the patient's behavior cause trouble? It is important to make sure that the behaviors are not linked to problems at home. For example, children who have experienced a serious life event, such as a divorce, a move, an illness, a change in school, or a death in the family, may act out or become forgetful.

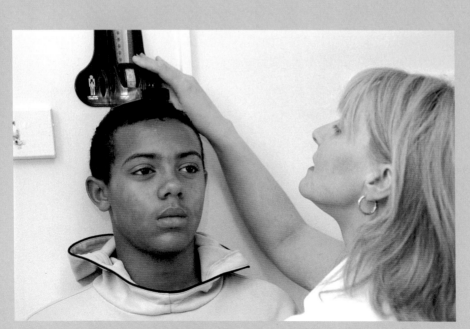

A physical exam can be a first step in diagnosing ADHD.

If the doctor suspects ADHD, he or she may recommend that a counselor, or a mental health specialist such as a psychiatrist or psychologist, see the patient. The specialist will ask more questions, looking for examples of inattentive behavior and hyperactive or impulsive behavior. The patient may be given psychological tests to evaluate memory, attention, and decision making.

Next, for children and teens, their teachers—both past and present—are asked to fill out a standard evaluation form on the patient's behavior in class. The specialist also needs to talk to the teachers, parents, and anyone else who knows the patient well, such as coaches or babysitters.

For adults, getting additional information about their behavior may be more complicated. The specialist talks with the patient to get a history of the current problem and childhood behavior that might point to ADHD symptoms. The parents can also provide information about the patient's childhood behavior. Memories of conflicts with other children, failure in school, punishments such as detentions, and frequent visits to the principal's office could be signs of ADHD in childhood. If school report cards are available, they may include comments such as "can't sit still," "doesn't pay attention in class," "does not work well in groups," or "not working up to potential." Interviews with people who are close to the patient, such as friends or a spouse, can also be helpful. Often adults with ADHD have problems at work and tend to get into driving accidents.

Here are some guidelines doctors use in diagnosing ADHD:

- ADHD behaviors first appeared before the person was seven years old.
- Behaviors are more serious and happen more often than in other children of the same age.
- Behaviors have continued for at least six months.
- Behaviors have created major difficulties in at least two areas of a person's life, such as school, work, home, or social settings with friends.

If a person has problems at school or work but behaves normally at home and with friends, he or she probably does not have ADHD.

Treating ADHD With Medicine

When ADHD is mentioned, many people immediately think of Ritalin. Ritalin is a medicine commonly used to treat ADHD. As many as 90 percent of children with ADHD are helped by Ritalin and other ADHD

Checklist for Diagnosing ADHD in Children

Hyperactive/Impulsive Behavior	Inattentive Behavior
✔ Fidgets a lot and has trouble sitting still.	✔ Often daydreams in class.
✔ Blurts out answers in class.	✔ Is easily distracted.
✔ Interrupts friends while they are speaking.	✔ Has trouble remembering the teacher's instructions.
✔ Has trouble waiting his or her turn in games or groups.	✔ Often loses or forgets his or her homework or books.
✔ Always seems to be "on the go." Runs around a lot or climbs on things when he or she is supposed to be sitting.	✔ Makes careless mistakes in schoolwork.
	✔ Doesn't listen to his or her parents when asked to do a task.
✔ Talks constantly.	✔ Has trouble sticking with a task until it is done.

medications.[4] These drugs can help adults with ADHD as well.

Ritalin is a stimulant, a drug that usually makes people feel more wide awake and full of energy. Stimulants do not make people with ADHD more hyper or active, though. Instead, the drug seems to calm them down. It helps them to pay attention and concentrate, so they are not as easily distracted. In people with ADHD, Ritalin makes dopamine more available to the brain cells.

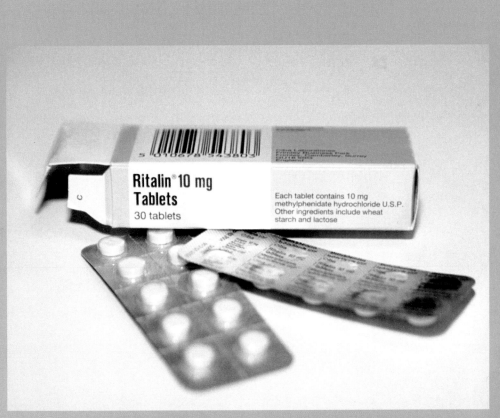

Doctors prescribe Ritalin for many adults and children with ADHD.

Ritalin belongs to a family of drugs called amphetamines. These drugs are strong stimulants that are available only with a doctor's prescription. They are controlled by strict laws because they are abused by some people who want to get a "high" (feelings of intense happiness and increased energy). When taken by people with ADHD, however, these drugs do not produce a high, as long as patients follow their doctor's directions. In 2007 the FDA approved a new amphetamine-type stimulant, Vyvanase, for the treatment of children with ADHD. This drug is less likely to be abused than other amphetamines because it does not produce much of a high.

Many people think that too many children are being treated with ADHD medications. They are frightened by the idea of giving kids a drug that they will take every day for many years. They worry that kids will become addicted to the drugs. However, there is no evidence that ADHD medications, taken in the prescribed doses, lead to drug abuse. In fact, long-term studies have shown that teenagers with ADHD who continued taking their medication through their teen years were less likely to abuse drugs than ADHD teens who were not taking medications.

Are ADHD Drugs Safe?

ADHD medications are safe and effective when taken under a doctor's care. However, stimulants are powerful drugs and they can have negative side effects. Some side effects may be annoying, such as irritability, headaches, increased anxiety, stomachaches, poor appetite, and sleep problems. A high dose of the drug could cause more alarming symptoms, such as increased heart rate and blood pressure, seizures (uncontrollable shaking), damage to the liver, mood changes, confusion, hallucinations, and irregular breathing. Doctors usually start with the lowest dose and then raise it gradually until it is just right. Sometimes a different drug may be more effective for a particular patient. These days, there are a number of ADHD medications from which to choose. Everybody is different. What works for one person may not work for another.

On the other hand, there are people who think Ritalin is a magic pill that can make ADHD disappear. When parents and teachers notice an improvement in the child's schoolwork and behavior, right away they consider the drug as some kind of cure. However, as yet, there is no cure for ADHD. Medications can only control the symptoms on the day they are taken. If the child forgets to take the medicine, the symptoms will return.

In 2003, the Food and Drug Administration (FDA) approved Strattera, the first nonstimulant treatment for

The ADHD Patch

In April 2006, the FDA approved the first skin patch to treat ADHD in children ages six to twelve. The ADHD patch, called Daytrana, is designed to be worn on the child's hip for nine hours. It releases the same stimulant that is in Ritalin. If there are any negative side effects, the patch can simply be removed. Currently this treatment is recommended only for children who have trouble swallowing pills or refuse to take them. Other kid-friendly choices include chewable tablets and a grape-flavored liquid.

ADHD. This drug raises the level of norepinephrine in the brain but can also produce serious side effects.

Doctors may prescribe antidepressants to ADHD patients who also suffer from depression. However, these drugs are not as effective as stimulants or Strattera in treating ADHD itself because they do not help to improve a person's attention span or concentration. Some antidepressants may also have dangerous side effects, including an increased risk for suicidal thoughts.

Behavior Modification

ADHD drugs help kids to pay attention and complete schoolwork, but they do not teach them how to behave in social situations. Adults with ADHD also need training in life skills, such as organizing their activities and getting along with others. That is why many mental health experts agree that ADHD should be treated with a combination of drugs and therapy. One type of therapy frequently used for people with ADHD is called behavior modification.

Behavior modification is a technique used to change a person's behavior. The parent, teacher, or mental health specialist sets goals for a child with ADHD. The adult then rewards good behavior and either ignores

Parents of kids with ADHD can reward good behavior with things like family outings.

inappropriate behavior or works with the child to correct it. There are three steps in this process.

1. Define the problem. If the problem is restlessness, for example, the child may be unable to sit still during dinner.

2. Set a reasonable goal. At first, it may be too hard for a child with ADHD to sit still until everyone in the family has finished eating. It is a good idea to break up the big goal into little goals that are easier to reach. For example, the child can try sitting still at the table for 5 minutes, then 10 minutes, then 15 minutes.

3. Work toward the goal. Most kids respond to rewards and consequences. Parents, teachers, and friends should praise the child whenever he or she makes some progress, even if the child does not achieve the goal. This will show that they are proud of the child's progress. Going to the movies or getting an ice cream cone may be used to reward reaching a goal. Discipline is also important. Kids need to know that there are consequences for their behaviors. The child should be told what kind of behavior is not acceptable, and what the consequences will be for those actions. A child who does not follow the rules will have a privilege taken away, such as playing video games or

Adults with ADHD can sometimes remember things better by writing notes or lists.

going out with friends. The kinds of rewards and consequences are adjusted as the child gets older.

For adults, a professional coach can help in developing more effective behaviors. Various tricks and props can be used. For example, a large calendar placed where it will be seen first thing in the morning can aid in remembering appointments, assignments, and personal goals. Writing lists and reminder notes is also helpful.

Having a special place to keep keys, wallet, bills, and paperwork can save a lot of time and stress from looking for things that are misplaced.

Counseling

Many children and adults with ADHD have low self-esteem. Psychological counseling can help them work through the past experiences that led to the feelings of worthlessness and develop a better self-image.

For treatment to be successful, children with ADHD need the support of their parents, teachers, and school counselors. Counselors can help children and family members learn about ADHD and how to cope with it. They can also talk to the children about their condition and help them feel better about themselves. They can help reduce the child's worries and anxieties. They can also teach the child how to handle specific situations at home, at school, or with friends.

Parents and teachers need to learn about ADHD so that they can understand what the child is going through. The more they know about ADHD, the more they can help kids achieve a positive, happy lifestyle. They can also learn ways to help a child change his or her behavior into something more acceptable.

Counselors can help children and their family members cope with ADHD.

ADHD at School

In 2004, Joanie Derry sued her son's school in Manatee County, Florida. The boy had been diagnosed with ADHD when he was in kindergarten, and a judge had told the school district to create a special education plan for him. The plan stated that the boy needed a chance to move around during class time, and that physical activity allowed him to get along with less medication. The teachers ignored the plan. In fact, they often punished the boy by keeping him in the classroom during recess and not allowing him to play with the other kids. They went back to court two more times before the school district finally agreed to enforce the special education plan.[5]

Many schools throughout the country do not have programs specifically for kids with ADHD. Most schools do have programs for children with learning disabilities, however. In some cases these kids are assigned to special classes. In others, kids with learning disabilities take most of their classes with the rest of their classmates and just go to special classes several hours a week. Parents who want more help for kids with attention problems have to hire tutors to work with them after school. There are also some summer programs and schools that give kids with ADHD the extra help they need.

It is very important for parents and teachers to have a lot of patience and understanding. They also need to work together and let each other know about progress and changes in the child's behavior. Friends and family members can help too. Treatment can be a long, frustrating process, but kids with ADHD usually try hard to get better.

For adults in particular, successful treatment of ADHD symptoms can be life-changing. After years of doing things in certain ways, it might be difficult to adjust to a new way of living. Patients may feel that by acting less impulsively, they have lost part of their personality. The therapist can help ADHD patients to adjust to the changes and encourage them to appreciate the accomplishments that result from better organization.

5

Living With ADHD

WHEN ROBERT JERGEN was a child, his mother used to call him "little monster" because he was always getting into trouble. He was constantly being scolded by his parents and teachers about something he did wrong. What they didn't realize was that Robert wasn't trying to be bad or naughty—he truly couldn't control his behavior.

As Robert got older, being a constant disappointment caused him to sink into depression a number of times. When he went to college, he turned to alcohol to quiet his "noisy" head. The alcohol helped him concentrate in class and get better grades. It also brought out years of pent-up anger, and after one out-of-control night in a bar, Robert knew he had to stop drinking. Once the drinking stopped, though, the noise in his head started up again.

After college, Robert got a job teaching adolescents with special needs. He loved working with the kids, but he was miserable dealing with the boring paperwork, long meetings, and coworkers constantly angry at the odd things he did or said. Robert's behavior was gradually becoming even more bizarre. One day, he poked a bald area on his boss's head and yelled, "Bald spot!"

Robert Jergen's mother called him "little monster" when he was a child. As an adult, Dr. Jergen wrote a book about growing up with ADHD. This photo appears on the cover of his book, *The Little Monster: Growing Up With ADHD.*

These words just popped out of his mouth without his even realizing it.

The turning point in Robert's life came when he was talking to one of his students, Troy. Troy had schizophrenia, and Robert was upset to find out that Troy had stopped taking his medication. Robert told Troy that he could be smart and successful if he took his pills every day. Suddenly it occurred to Robert that maybe there was a drug that could improve *his* life.

Robert went to a number of therapy sessions. He also had a functional MRI test taken. This imaging test showed abnormal brain activity. However, doctors could not determine from the MRI whether he had ADHD. One day, Robert went to a support group meeting for adults with learning difficulties. Someone there described what it felt like to live with ADHD: "My mind is like a wall of television sets, each on a different channel, and I don't have the remote." For the first time, Robert felt that someone could relate to what he was going through. "One second I thought that I was a loser. A freak," he said. "The next moment I knew that I had ADHD. I wasn't alone."[1]

For the next two years, Robert was prescribed various ADHD medications, but he stopped taking them because they caused too many negative side effects. He then decided to come up with his own little tricks to control his condition. He started by keeping a journal that showed when and where he got the most work done. That way he could create an environment that would get rid of distractions and allow him to stay focused. For example, Robert keeps his office dimly lit with just a single bright light shining on his computer. The spotlight on his computer reminds him to pay attention. He plays soft music in the background to block outside distractions so that he can relax and concentrate. He also keeps a laptop nearby with a computer game running. He switches to that for a few seconds if his mind starts to wander. When his mind gets in a fog, he hops on his treadmill until he breaks a sweat. This short burst of exercise usually helps to clear his mind so that he can focus again.

Most importantly, Robert has a strong support system. He met a very encouraging teacher who helped him a great deal when he went back to school for his Ph.D. Now he is married, and his wife helps to keep him on track. She reminds him to take a walk when he gets angry or frustrated. This support system has helped to rebuild Robert's self-esteem after years of feeling like a failure.

Robert still cannot control his behavior at times, but he has learned how to make his life more manageable. He has written a book about growing up with ADHD. He has also been coming up with techniques that he hopes will someday help other people with ADHD manage their condition without medication.[2]

There are a number of things that people with ADHD can do to help them listen better, remember things better, and get things done. In fact, the helpful hints on the following pages are good for anybody who has trouble paying attention at times, forgets things, and is not very organized.

ADHD and Driving

Teenagers who have ADHD have more traffic accidents than those without the condition. When it comes to driving, avoiding distractions is *very* important. That means not driving with a carload of friends, not talking on your cell phone while driving, and not getting distracted by loud music in the car. Driving with an adult in the car, even after getting your license, may also help keep you focused.

What You Can Do at Home

- Write notes to yourself. Colored sticky notes are great because you can stick them anywhere.

- If your mom or dad wants you to do something, ask them to write a note so that you won't forget.

- Use a calendar to keep track of places you have to go. Make sure to check the calendar every morning.

- Try to do tasks right away. If you put them off until later, you might forget about them.

- If you have to go somewhere at a certain time, set the kitchen timer. For instance, if you have to get ready for soccer practice in a half hour, set the timer for thirty minutes.

- Do your homework in a quiet place that is away from distractions, such as a TV or siblings.

- When you finish your homework, always put your schoolbooks in the same special place so that you won't have to hunt for them in the morning.

- Before you go to bed, decide what clothes you will wear the next day. Place your shoes beside them. That way you won't have to rush around in the morning.

- Develop a morning routine. For example: go to the bathroom, take a shower, get dressed, eat breakfast, brush your teeth, get your books, and go to school.

What You Can Do at School

- Use a student planner. Write down homework assignments and projects, along with their due dates.

- Sit near the front of the classroom, and look at the teacher when he or she is talking.

- Work on one thing at a time. Keep your desk clear of everything else.

- Don't sit next to talkative kids.

- Wear a loose-fitting rubber band on your wrist. If you start to daydream, give it a little snap.

- Do not bring a music player or handheld games to school. They can distract you.

- If you don't understand something in class, ask the teacher for help.

- Participate in class. Raise your hand to ask questions and make comments. This will help to make the class more interesting.

How to Get Along With Friends

- Share your stuff with friends.

- Take turns. Everybody should have a chance to play during a game.

- Stay calm. Don't get overly excited or too loud.

- Before you talk, listen to be sure no one else is already talking. That way, you will not interrupt other people's conversations.

- Compliment your friends when they do something well, and thank them when they help you.

- Don't make fun of other people. They do not like it any more than you do.

- If you feel angry, don't hit, yell, or call names. Walk away and calm down so that you won't say or do something you will feel bad about later.

- Say you're sorry if you have said or done something that hurts someone's feelings.

6

ADHD
and the Future

MANY PEOPLE SAY that kids today spend too much time playing computer games. That could explain why more and more kids are having a hard time staying focused on tasks away from the computer, such as in the classroom or sitting at the dinner table. Whether or not that is true, special computer game systems have been designed to help children with ADHD to focus better.

Eight-year-old Zac Blackwell got a chance to try out one of these systems, the Attention Trainer, in the summer of 2000. He was one of several children chosen to test this product. Zac's mother was hoping that the program would help her son focus his attention better.

Zac had a lot of trouble behaving at school and at home. His pediatrician felt that Zac was too young to have ADHD, but Mrs. Blackwell disagreed. When she heard about the new computer program, she was relieved to find something that could possibly help her son.

To play Attention Trainer, Zac had to wear a bicycle-like helmet lined with sensors that track the brain's activity. As the sensors measure the level of attention, the information is transmitted to the software in the game. The amount of action in the game depends on

This boy is playing a computer game called "Play Attention" to help his concentration.

how much attention the player gives to it. For example, in a game called Breakaway Racer, the bicycle rider speeds up when the player concentrates. Attention Trainer also includes a 3-D version of the classic Pong game, based on table tennis. As the player learns to concentrate, the paddle gets bigger and bigger.

During the summer, Zac played Attention Trainer twice a week. After he returned to school, his mother noticed a definite change in her son's behavior: "My child tells me he now knows what it feels like to focus, and I can see the difference in both his schoolwork and in social settings," his mother said.[1]

After Zac completed the program, he was given a free game system by the company. He continued to play Attention Trainer about three to four times a week. Some experts are not convinced that the computer system actually helps, but Mrs. Blackwell believes it does. She noticed that when Zac's Attention Trainer was not working for about a week, he was starting to return to his old behaviors. After the machine was fixed, Zac soon got his focus back.[2]

For decades, drugs have been the main focus in treating ADHD. However, there are concerns over the long-term effects of ADHD drugs. Therefore, people are starting to turn to a variety of alternative methods of treatment. These new methods can be used in addition to the standard treatments to make them more effective. They also provide harmless treatment choices for parents who don't want to give their children drugs and for kids who have had bad reactions to the medications.

Training the Brain

Systems such as Attention Trainer are based on neurofeedback, a technique that has been used for years to help improve the concentration of astronauts and Olympic athletes. Neurofeedback is designed to help people train certain parts of their brain. In ADHD, for example, people who have trouble focusing use neurofeedback to change their brain-wave patterns in the frontal lobe to increase their concentration.

How does neurofeedback work? Scientists can determine a person's state of mind by the type of wave pattern in certain parts of the brain. These patterns can be measured and recorded in an electroencephalogram (EEG). There are five main types of brain wave patterns:

Beta waves are the fastest brain waves. A person who is focused has a lot of beta waves.

SMR waves are a type of beta wave. They are observed when a person is mentally preparing for a challenging physical activity. (*SMR* stands for *sensorimotor* cortex, the part of the brain involved in body senses and muscle movements.)

Alpha waves are slower. They occur during relaxation.

Theta waves are even slower. They occur when a person is daydreaming or is very close to falling asleep.

Delta waves are the slowest brain waves. They occur when a person is in a deep sleep.

Normally, the amount of beta waves increases when a person tries to concentrate. This doesn't happen in a person with ADHD. Instead, the amount of theta waves—the daydreaming brain wave—increases. Instead of focusing, people with ADHD space out.

The goal of neurofeedback is to train the brain to increase the beta waves in the brain and decrease the theta waves. The technique uses a reward system to get the desired effect. In Attention Trainer, for example, the player's increased attention in the Pong game is rewarded by increasing the size of the paddles.

Some researchers have criticized the neurofeedback approach, saying that the case studies do not prove anything because they were not properly controlled. In issues of *Attention Research Update* from 2003 and 2006,[3] however, Duke University researcher David Rabiner discussed a number of case study reports and controlled studies showing positive results. For example, one study reported in 2002 involved 100 children diagnosed with ADHD. Half of them received the usual combination of stimulant drugs, behavior therapy, and school counseling services. The other half used neuro-feedback systems in addition to the standard treatments. A year later, all the children were evaluated according to psychological tests and questionnaires filled out by their parents and teachers. All of the children in the program showed improvement of their ADHD symptoms at the end of the year of treatment. Then the stimulant medicines were stopped for a week, and the tests and questionnaires were repeated. After the children had been off their medication, only those who had neurofeedback training still showed improved behavior.[4]

Brain Exercises

Can learning to juggle or to balance on one leg help kids with ADHD? Some experts think so. Brain Gym centers

Children in India do exercises to improve their concentration. Here they participate in a competition solving math problems.

in Seattle and other U.S. cities teach kids movements that help develop coordination and train different parts of the brain to work together. These exercises and those taught at Dore Achievement Centers are aimed at stimulating the cerebellum, a region in the lower back of the brain. Scientists have long known that the cerebellum helps to control and coordinate movements. Brain scans that show the brain in action, however, have revealed that this part of the brain is also involved in attention and the processing of language and music. The Dore program typically takes about a year. Kids with learning difficulties are first tested, then prescribed sets of exercises designed to help them. Every six weeks, they come back to the center for more testing and a new set of exercise prescriptions.

Like many other ADHD specialists, Massachusetts child psychologist Edward Hallowell was doubtful about the benefits claimed for non-drug treatments. In fact, he laughed when he first heard about the Dore method. His son Jack has ADHD. Drugs had helped Jack, but he still hated reading. Hallowell decided to give the Dore method a try. The results were dramatic. After three months on the program, Jack began looking forward to reading at night. Hallowell says that researchers are right to be doubtful about new methods that have not been thoroughly studied and tested— especially those that could be harmful, such as taking a new drug. However, some of them, such as those that modify behavior, may be helpful.[5]

Training the Ear

Another promising approach targets listening skills. The Tomatis Method is a technique that was developed by a French ear, nose, and throat specialist, Dr. Alfred A. Tomatis. It uses music at different frequencies to retrain the way people with ADHD listen to and hear sounds.[6] Scientific studies on children with learning disabilities and behavior problems have shown that the Tomatis Method can help them to improve their social and academic skills and increase their attention span. A detailed analysis of five studies, published in 1999 in the *International Journal of Hearing*, found that this method

Tammy McGraw

SPOTLIGHT
Dancing With ADHD

Education specialist Tammy McGraw has been conducting a study that is going to make kids with ADHD want to dance—that is, to Dance Dance Revolution (DDR). The study, reported in 2004, suggests that this popular music video game may help kids with ADHD to read better by training them to focus and pay attention. To play the game, kids move to a musical beat as they stomp down on four or more large panels with arrows, trying to match steps displayed on an animated computer screen. Educators have called the game a cross between two classic children's games, Twister and Simon Says.

McGraw got the idea to study DDR after she noticed a long line of kids outside a mall. Curious to see what all the excitement was about, she was surprised to discover that they were all waiting for a chance to dance with the popular computer program. She remembered reading about research suggesting that activities involving visual and rhythmic stimulation could help kids with reading and attention problems. She thought that perhaps the DDR video game craze could be used in treating ADHD.

McGraw and her team studied about fifty sixth-graders who were can also be helpful for people with ADHD.[7] They have difficulty sifting through all the stimuli in their environment. (Stimuli can be anything that demands attention—a conversation, a running dog, hot water, the sound of glass hitting the floor.) In the Tomatis Method,

diagnosed with ADHD. They all started by taking a series of reading tests. Then half of the children were told to play DDR for about an hour each week. The other group was told to continue with their normal routine.

Three months later, all the kids took the same reading tests again. In most areas, the scores seemed basically the same for both groups. However, the kids who played Dance Dance Revolution did somewhat better in tests involving memorizing and immediately recalling a word or series of numbers. The more times they played the game, the better they did on these tests. DDR dancers must match their movements to the visual images and music. They are training the parts of the brain involved in paying attention, remembering, and coordinating movements.

McGraw believes that DDR and other video games are a great learning tool because they are something exciting that kids are drawn to. She is encouraged by the results so far, but she says more research must be done before any definite conclusions can be drawn.[8]

people with ADHD can learn how to concentrate on certain sounds while tuning out background noise. This allows them to focus on stimuli that involve other senses, as well.

It can take many weeks for people to learn how to control which sounds they listen to, but the results can be dramatic. One mother commented, for example, that she couldn't believe the change in her son after he completed the listening training program. She explains, "It used to take two hours to get out the door in the morning and now Paul is ready before I am. We're not fighting over homework, and there are many days now when he gets it done himself. Our family life is totally different."[9]

Diet and Exercise

What you eat can have an effect on how well your brain works. Even though ADHD is not caused by eating too many sugary foods, a healthy diet provides the body with important nutrients that help to keep your brain connections strong. In fact, studies have shown that kids do better at school when they eat a nutritious breakfast. Eating a substantial amount of protein at breakfast is especially helpful. It supplies

Green Time

Could a stroll through the woods be good for your mental health? Possibly. In a national study, spending time in nature—"green time"—helped to reduce ADHD symptoms in children ages 5 to 18. Four hundred fifty-two children with ADHD were studied.

During the study, the kids participated in activities that took place in three different settings: indoors; outdoors without much greenery, such as in parking lots; and outdoors in greener areas, such as parks, backyards, and tree-lined streets. Parents kept track of and recorded their children's behaviors after activities. Later, researchers concluded that children who spent time in nature were calmer and could concentrate better. They also had less trouble following directions and completing tasks. For example, playing outside in backyards or in open fields reduced ADHD symptoms much more than playing inside in the gym or playing basketball outside on paved surfaces. "Green time" may allow a reduction in a child's medication. It is also helpful for children who cannot take ADHD drugs.[10]

building materials for the formation of new brain connections and is also a longer-lasting source of energy than carbohydrates (sugars).

You may have heard that fish is good "brain food." That's because it contains omega-3 fatty acids, which belong to a healthy group of fats. Salmon, tuna, and sardines contain large amounts of omega-3 and are very important in a person's diet. Studies have shown that kids who don't get enough omega-3 fatty acids in their diet are much more likely to be hyperactive, have learning disabilities, and have behavior difficulties. In addition, eating too many foods loaded with saturated fats (the unhealthy fats) may actually interfere with the body's ability to use the omega-3 fatty acids. (Foods such as potato chips, cheeseburgers, pizza, and frosted cupcakes are all high in saturated fats.)

Exercise is good not only for the body, but for the mind as well. Researchers have found that physical activity increases the levels of the two important neurotransmitters—dopamine and norepinephrine— that help people calm down and focus. Many people with ADHD find exercise helpful in managing their condition. Fifteen-year-old Kat Orlov, for example, used to spend four hours a day trying to finish her homework because of her disorder. Then she signed up for the crew team and started working out a couple of hours every day. She still takes ADHD medication, but exercise has helped a great deal: "When I exercise," she says, "I feel much more energized and awake. I have more of a feeling to sit down and get something finished."[11] Now it takes her half the time to do her homework.

Exercise can also help ease depression and anxiety. When the body is active, chemicals called endorphins

Exercise can improve a person's focus.

work in the brain to produce "happy" feelings. Exercise can also make people feel good about themselves, giving them a sense of accomplishment, strength, and independence.

Although many of these approaches have shown promising results, much more research still needs to be done. In the meantime, many kids and adults have found success in drug treatments and behavior therapy. For these people, finally having some control over their lives has made a world of difference.

Questions and Answers

Can eating too much candy give me ADHD? Eating too many sweets does not cause ADHD. The sugar in candy could give you a burst of energy for a while, but after it wears off, you're back to your old self. ADHD is a condition that you have all the time, whether you eat sweets or not.

Is ADHD a *real* problem, or is it just an excuse to misbehave? According to the American Psychiatric Association, ADHD is an official medical condition. There is a problem in the way the brain works. Treatment can help people with ADHD control their behavior better.

There's a kid in my class who is always getting into trouble. Could he have ADHD? Possibly, but there are a lot of reasons why a kid could be acting up in class. He could be reacting to a tough family life, or he may feel insecure and need attention. Teachers, counselors, and mental health professionals can work together to make a proper diagnosis.

I'm confused. Is it ADD or ADHD? I hear people use both terms. Which is it? ADHD is a general term that includes three types of attention disorders. One of them is ADD. ADD includes symptoms of inattention, but not hyperactivity.

My parents think that my sister might have ADD. Is that possible? Only boys get that, right? No. Boys are three times more likely than girls to be diagnosed with ADHD. That's because many of them have hyperactive symptoms, which are easy to notice. Girls are more likely to have ADD. They may go unnoticed because they typically sit quietly and daydream.

My brother was just diagnosed with ADHD. I heard that it runs in the family. Does that mean that I have it, too? Your brother inherited genes for ADHD, which means it is possible—but not certain—that you have it, too. You should also be evaluated by a mental health professional.

Can kids grow out of ADHD? Some children do grow out of it. Hyperactivity, in particular, tends to decrease as a child gets older. However, many kids with ADHD will still have problems with attention and organization when they are adults.

Growing up, I always felt like I was stupid. I had such a hard time learning things in class compared to everyone else. Recently, at age 22, I was diagnosed with ADHD. Does that mean I'm not stupid after all? People with ADHD are not stupid. In fact, most of them have average or above average intelligence. There are many people with ADHD who are doctors, lawyers, teachers, artists, writers, inventors, and pro sports players.

ADHD Timeline

1845 ..... German doctor Heinrich Hoffmann publishes "The Story of Fidgety Philip," the first accurate description of a child with ADHD.

1902 ..... English pediatrician George Still documents a number of cases involving impulsiveness. He believes the cause is medical rather than psychological.

1917–1918 ..... An encephalitis outbreak leaves patients with ADHD-like symptoms. Doctors later use the term *brain damaged* to describe all hyperactive children.

1937 ..... Dr. Charles Bradley discovers that stimulants work to calm down hyperactive children.

1955 ..... The Food and Drug Administration (FDA) approves Ritalin to treat psychological disorders.

1960 ..... New York child psychiatrist Stella Chess coins the term *Hyperactive Child Syndrome*. She believes that hyperactivity is *not* caused by brain damage, but that something is abnormal in the brain.

1967 .... Ritalin is prescribed specifically to treat children with ADHD.

1970s .... ADHD is identified in adults.

1973 .... Dr. Benjamin F. Feingold claims that hyperactivity is caused by an overload of sugar and food additives in the diet.

1980 .... The American Psychiatric Association officially names the condition attention deficit disorder (ADD).

1990 .... Dr. Alan Zametkin, and a team of National Institute of Mental Health (NIMH) researchers, discover that brain activity is different in people with ADD than in those without ADD.

1994 .... The American Psychiatric Association renames the disorder attention-deficit/ hyperactivity disorder (ADHD) to include behaviors with or without hyperactivity.

1996 .... The World Health Organization (WHO) warns overuse of Ritalin has reached dangerous proportions.

1999 .... Results from the largest study of ADHD treatment to date, known as the Multimodal Treatment Study of Children with Attention-Deficit/ Hyperactivity Disorder (MTA Study), is published in the *American Journal of Psychiatry*.

2001	The International Consensus Statement on ADHD, containing the signatures of more than 80 of the world's ADHD experts, reports that ADHD is a medical condition and can be treated with medication just like other mental disorders.
2003	The FDA approves Strattera, the first nonstimulant treatment for ADHD.
2006	The FDA approves the first skin patch (Daytrana) to treat ADHD in children ages six to twelve.
2007	The FDA approves a new stimulant drug for ADHD, Vyvanase, which is less likely to be abused than other amphetamine-type stimulants.

For More Information

Attention Deficit Disorder Association (ADDA)
15000 Commerce Parkway, Suite C
Mount Laurel, NJ 08054
Phone: 856-439-9099
Fax: 856-439-0525
Web site: http://www.add.org

Centers for Disease Control and Prevention
1600 Clifton Road
Atlanta, GA 30333
Toll-free: 800-311-3435
Web site: ADHD Home,
http://www.cdc.gov/ncbddd/adhd/

Children and Adults with Attention-deficit/Hyperactivity
Disorder (CHADD)
8181 Professional Place, Suite 150
Landover, MD 20785
Toll-free: 1-800-233-4050
Fax: 301-306-7090
Web site: http://www.chadd.org and
http://www.help4adhd.org (National Resource Center
on ADHD)

Dore Achievement Centers
P.O. Box 50
Lake Arrowhead, CA 92352
Toll-free: (877) 855-3673
Website: http://www.doreusa.com

Learning Disabilities Association of America
4156 Library Road
Pittsburgh, PA 15234-1349
Phone: 412-341-1515
Fax: 412-344-0224
Web site: http://www.idanatl.org

National Institute of Mental Health (NIMH)
Public Information and Communications Branch
6001 Executive Boulevard, Room 8184, MSC 9663
Bethesda, MD 20892-9663
Toll-free: 1-866-615-6464
E-mail: nimhinfo@nih.gov
Web site: http://www.nimh.nih.gov

Camps & Schools Serving People with ADHD and Special Needs
http://adhd.kids.tripod.com/camp.html
This list includes:
Landmark College in Putney, VT
Pima Academy in Tucson, AZ
Stone Mountain School at Camp Elliott in Black Mountain, NC
Vail Valley Learning Camp in Vail, CO

Chapter Notes

Chapter 1. Out of Control

1. Patty Rasmussen, "Q&A with Adam LaRoche," *ChopTalk Magazine*, August 29, 2006, <http://atlanta.braves.mlb.com/NASApp/mlb/news/article.jsp?ymd=20060829&content_id=1634633&vkey=news_atl&fext=.jsp&c_id=atl> (August 31, 2006).

2. R. Travis Haney, "Atlanta's LaRoche Continues to Fight Battle with ADD," *Augusta Chronicle*, August 6, 2006, <http://chronicle.augusta.com/stories/080606/bra_91599.shtml> (August 31, 2006).

3. Rasmussen.

4. Rasmussen; Haney.

5. National Institute of Mental Health, "Attention Deficit Hyperactivity Disorder," updated February 17, 2006, <http://www.nimh.nih.gov/publicat/adhd.cfm> (September 8, 2006).

Chapter 2. The History of ADHD

1. National Institute of Mental Health, "Attention Deficit Hyperactivity Disorder," updated February 17, 2006, <http://www.nimh.nih.gov/publicat/adhd.cfm> (September 8, 2006).

2. Edward M. Hallowell and John J. Ratey, *Driven to Distraction* (New York: Pantheon Books, 1994), pp. 270–271.

3. Russell A. Barkley, *Attention-Deficit Hyperactivity Disorder: A Handbook for Diagnosis and Treatment*, Second Edition (New York: Guilford Press, 1998), pp. 3–4.

4. Stella Chess, "Diagnosis and Treatment of the Hyperactive Child," *New York State Journal of Medicine*, vol. 60, 1960, p. 2379.

5. Ibid./pp. 2379–2381.

6. International Food Information Council Foundation, "Taking the Hype Out of Hyperactivity," *KidSource Online*, Winter 1988, <http://www.kidsource.com/kidsource/content3/ific/ific.hyper.foods.k12.3.html> (September 22, 2006).

7. National Institute of Mental Health.

8. National Institute of Mental Health, "NIMH Research on Treatment for Attention Deficit Hyperactivity Disorder (ADHD): The Multimodal Treatment Study—Questions and Answers," March 2000, <http://www.nimh.nih.gov/childhp/mtaqa.cfm> (September 22, 2006); David Rabiner, "New Results from the MTA Study—Do Treatment Effects Persist?" June 2004, <http://www.helpforadd.com/2004/june.htm> (September 27, 2006).

Chapter 3. What Is ADHD?

1. Dav Pilkey, "The Almost Completely True Adventures of Dav Pilkey," *Dav Pilkey's Extra Crunchy WebSite O'Fun* <http://www.pilkey.com/adv-text.php> (September 26, 2006).

2. Deirdre Donahue, " 'Captain Underpants' Jockeys for Attention," *USA Today*, August 20, 2003, <http://www.usatoday.com/life/books/reviews/2003-08-20-captain-underpants_x.htm> (September 26, 2006).

3. National Mental Health Association, "Attention-Deficit/Hyperactivity Disorder (ADHD)," © 2006, <http://www.nmha.org/children/children_mh_matters/adhd.cfm> (September 29, 2006).

4. Lindá Bren, "ADHD: Not Just for Kids Anymore," *FDA Consumer*, November–December 2004, p. 15.

5. Children and Adults with Attention-Deficit/ Hyperactivity Disorder (CHADD), "AD/HD and Coexisting Conditions: Disruptive Behavior Disorders," © 2005, <http://www.help4adhd.org/documents/WWK5b3.pdf> (October 3, 2006).

Chapter 4. Diagnosis and Treatment

1. Carla Garnett, "Attention Deficit, Hyperactivity Explored in Depth at Step Forum," *NIH Record*, February 24, 2006, <http://www.nih.gov/nihrecord02_242006/story01.htm> (August 29, 2006).

2. Ibid.

3. Molly Zametkin, "Growing Up with ADD—A Personal Perspective," *The ADHD Report*, August 2006, pp. 14–16.

4. Aribert Rothenberger and Tobias Banaschewski, "Informing the ADHD Debate," *Scientific American Mind*, December 2004. <http://www.sciammind.com/article.cfm?articleID=000C6D64-1995-1196-906983414B7F0000> (October 9, 2006); Margaret Strock, *Attention Deficit Hyperactivity Disorder*, National Institute of Mental Health, 2006, <http://www.nimh.nih.gov/publicat/NIMHadhdpub.pdf> (May 16, 2007).

5. Tiffany Lankes, "ADHD Putting Strain on Schools," Sarasota, FL, *Herald-Tribune*, June 27, 2004, <http://www.heraldtribune.com/apps/pbcs.dll/article?AID=/20040627/NEWS/60127007> (March 8, 2007); Tiffany Lankes, "Schools Close to Settling Mom's ADHD Suit," Sarasota, FL, *Herald-Tribune*, October 28, 2005,

<http://www.heraldtribune.com/apps/pbcs.dll/article?AID= /20051028/NEWS/510280489> (March 8, 2007).

Chapter 5. Living With ADHD

1. Joseph Biederman, "Turning Adult ADHD Around," July 12, 2005, *Play Attention: Attention Deficit*, <http:// www.playattention.com/attention-deficit/articles/turning-adult-adhd-around/> (October 10, 2006).

2. Ibid.

Chapter 6. ADHD and the Future

1. Simon Hensby, "NASA Technology to Help ADDers?" February 14, 2001, *ADDers.org—ADD/ADHD News*, <http://www.adders.org/news37. htm> (October 17, 2006).

2. Ibid.; Bonnie Rothman Morris, "Gadget Tries to Lengthen Young Attention Spans," *The New York Times*, February 8, 2001, p. G8.

3. David Rabiner, "The Role of Neurofeedback in the Treatment of ADHD," *Attention Research Update: January 2003*, <http://www.helpforadd.com/2003/january.htm> (February 23, 2007); David Rabiner, "New Controlled Study Shows that Neurofeedback Helps Children Pay Attention and Improves Their Brain Function," © 2007, <http://www.peakachievement.com/articles/Article— Neurofeedback%20for%20Training%20Childrens%20 Attention.htm> (February 23, 2007).

4. Ibid.

5. Anne Marie Chaker, "Attention Deficit Gets New Approach," *The Wall Street Journal*, April 5, 2005, p. D4.

6. Pierre Sollier, "Finding Solutions That Offer Hope and Confidence," *ADD & ADHD*, © 2001–2006, <http://www.

tomatis.com/English/Articles/add_adhd.html> (May 17, 2007).

7. Pierre Sollier, "Research," *The Tomatis Method*, © 2001–2006, <http://www.tomatis.com/English/Articles/research.html> (February 27, 2007); Tim Gilmor, "The Efficacy of the Tomatis Method for Children with Learning and Communication Disorders," *International Journal of Listening*, Vol. 13, p. 12 (1999).

8. Tammy M. McGraw, Krista Burdette, and Kristine Chadwick, "The Effects of a Consumer-Oriented Multimedia Game on the Reading Disorders of Children with ADHD," *Edvantia*, 2004, <http://www.edvantia.org/publications/pdf/04Multimedia_ADHD.pdf> (October 20, 2006); Eric Sabo, "Get Out! Popular Dance Video Game Helps Kids with ADHD," *Riley Hospital for Children*, July 7, 2005, <http://rileyhospital.healthology.com/focus_article.asp?b=rileyhospital&f=children&c=adhd_videogames&spg=FLA> (October 20, 2006).

9. Valerie Dejean, "Attention Deficit Disorders (ADD/ADHD)," *Spectrum Center Method*, © 2006, <http://www.spectrumcenter.net/addadhd.html> (October 16, 2006).

10. Frances E. Kuo and Andrea Faber Taylor, "A Potential Natural Treatment for Attention-Deficit/Hyperactivity Disorder: Evidence From a National Study," *American Journal of Public Health*, Vol 94, no. 9, September 2004, pp. 1580–1586.

11. Liz Szabo, "ADHD Treatment Is Getting a Workout," *USA Today.com*, March 26, 2006, <http://www.usatoday.com/news/health/2006-03-26-adhd-treatment_x.htm> (October 11, 2006).

Glossary

amphetamine—A type of stimulant drug that is sometimes abused to get a "high" (feelings of intense happiness and increased energy). The amphetamines used for ADHD are not addictive when taken in the prescribed doses.

antidepressants—Drugs used to treat depression.

anxiety disorder—A condition that causes stress and panic.

attention deficit disorder (ADD)—A condition characterized by an inability to concentrate, pay attention, and/or control one's actions.

attention-deficit/hyperactivity disorder (ADHD)—A term used to describe attention disorders with or without hyperactivity.

behavior modification—A treatment often used to change unacceptable behavior in people with ADHD.

cerebellum—A region at the lower back of the brain. It helps to control and coordinate movements and is also involved in attention and the processing of language and music.

cerebral cortex—The outermost layer of the brain. We use it to think, remember, make decisions, and control the movements of the body.

coexisting conditions—A disorder that occurs in addition to another condition.

combined type—A type of ADHD in which a person

shows both inattentive and hyperactive-impulsive symptoms.

depression—A condition that causes severe sadness and hopelessness.

distractible—Having an attention that is easily turned to something else.

dopamine—A neurotransmitter chemical that works in the brain to help control behavior.

frontal lobe—The part of the brain that helps a person concentrate, make plans, and think before acting.

gene—Hereditary material inside body cells that carries information about a person's characteristics.

hyperactive—Restless, unable to concentrate for any length of time, having a need for continual physical activity.

hyperactive-impulsive type—A kind of ADHD combining both hyperactivity (restlessness, inability to concentrate) and impulsivity (acting before thinking).

impulsivity—Acting before thinking.

inattentive type—A kind of ADHD in which the person has difficulty paying attention.

inherited—Passed on by genes from parents to children.

learning disability—A condition that makes certain areas of learning difficult, such as reading, written expression, or mathematics.

neurofeedback—A technique that monitors brain-wave patterns and rewards changes in behavior, leading to a desirable result.

neurotransmitter—A chemical that carries messages from one part of the brain to another.

norepinephrine—A neurotransmitter chemical that works in the brain to block distractions and focus attention.

PCBs (polychlorinated biphenyls)—Industrial chemicals commonly found in water and air pollution.

positron-emission tomography (PET) scan—A test in which a radioactive substance is injected into a patient and then tracked as it travels through the arteries of the body.

receptor—A protein on the surface of a cell that picks up particular kinds of neurotransmitters, hormones, or other chemicals.

Ritalin—A drug (methylphenidate) used to treat ADHD.

self-esteem—How you feel about yourself.

stimulant—A drug that makes a body system more active, making most people feel more alert and energetic.

stimuli—Things in the environment that attract attention or produce mental or physical reactions.

toxin—A poison.

Further Reading

Ashley, Susan. *The ADD & ADHD Answer Book*. Naperville, IL: Sourcebooks, Inc., 2005.

Dendy, Chris A. Zeigler, and Alex Zeigler. *A Bird's Eye View of Life with ADD and ADHD: Advice from Young Survivors*. Queensland, Australia: Cherish the Children, 2003.

Fox, Janet S. *Get Organized Without Losing It*. Minneapolis, MN: Free Spirit Publishing, Inc., 2006.

Joffe, Vera, and Monica Iachan. *A Day in the Life of an Adult with ADHD*. Coral Springs, FL: Vera Joffe, Ph.D., P.A., 2006.

Nadeau, Kathleen G., and Ellen B. Dixon. *Learning to Slow Down and Pay Attention*. Washington, DC: Magination Press, 2004.

Quinn, Patricia O. *50 Activities and Games for Kids with ADHD*. Washington, DC: Magination Press, 2000.

Quinn, Patricia O., and Judith M. Stern. *Putting on the Brakes*. Washington, DC: Magination Press, 2001.

Strong, Jeff, and Michael O. Flanagan. *AD/HD for Dummies*. Hoboken, NJ: Wiley Publishing, Inc., 2005.

Taylor, John F. *The Survival Guide for Kids with ADD or ADHD*. Minneapolis, MN: Free Spirit Publishing, Inc., 2006.

Trueit, Trudi Strain. *ADHD*. New York: Franklin Watts, 2004.

Internet Addresses

(See also **For More Information**, p. 98)

National Institute of Mental Health. *Attention Deficit Hyperactivity Disorder.*
<http://www.nimh.nih.gov/publicat/adhd.cfm>

ADDitude. *Living Well with ADD and Learning Disabilities.*
<http://www.additudemag.com/>

National Resource Center on ADHD.
<http://www. help4adhd.org/>

Index